Becoming A Healthy Disciple
Small Group Study & Worship Guide

Also by Stephen A. Macchia

Becoming a Healthy Church: Ten Traits of a Vital Ministry
Becoming a Healthy Church Workbook
Becoming a Healthy Disciple
Becoming a Healthy Team: Five Traits of Vital Leadership
Becoming a Healthy Team Exercises
Crafting A Rule of Life

Becoming A Healthy Disciple
Small Group Study & Worship Guide

A leader and participant guide for use with *Becoming a Healthy Disciple*.

By Stephen A. Macchia

LEADERSHIP
TRANSFORMATIONS INC.
FORMATION | DISCERNMENT | RENEWAL

Published by Leadership Transformations
P.O. Box 338, Lexington, MA 02420
www.leadershiptransformations.org

Second printing, March 2014
Printed in the United States of America

Library of Congress Cataloging-in-Publication Data

Macchia, Stephen A., 1956–
    Becoming a healthy disciple: Small group study & worship guide / Stephen A. Macchia
        p.   cm.
    Includes bibliographical references.
    ISBN-13: 978-06159-9235-8
    ISBN-10: 0615992358
    1. Christian life. 2. Spiritual life—Christianity. I. Title.
BV4501.3.M22 2004
248.4—dc22   2003021509

Small Group Study and Worship Guide is a complementary text of Stephen A. Macchia's book: *Becoming a Healthy Disciple*, Leadership Transformations, 2013.

Reflective readings by Rueben P. Job are taken from: Job, Rueben P. and Shawchuck, Norman. *A Guide to Prayer for All Who Seek God,* Nashville: Upper Room Books, 2003. All rights reserved.

Hymns taken from *The Celebration Hymnal: Songs and Hymns for Worship.* Copyright 1997, Word Music/Integrity Music. All rights reserved.

Brief introductions to each of the ten traits have also been printed as devotionals published by Words of Hope, Grand Rapids, MI. (www.woh.org)

Scripture quotations noted are NIV and are taken from the Holy Bible, New International Version. Copyright 1973, 1978, and 1984 by International Bible Society. Used by permission of Zondervan Bible Publishing House. All rights reserved.

For Ruth, Nathan, and Rebekah
With all my love and gratitude

Contents

Foreword

Becoming a Healthy Disciple is a life-long journey. The traits that lead to spiritual health and vitality are comprehensive…they impact the overall life of a thoughtful believer. Developing the heart and skills we are called to embody are best formulated over time and within the context of authentic community.

From over three and a half decades of ministry, I have discovered that the safety of a small group of like-minded, like-hearted Christians is the best place to process our spiritual growth. When we entrust our lives into the hands of loving and caring "siblings" in the faith, we discover true joy in our journey toward maturity.

This study and worship guide has been designed with the needs of a small group in mind. My prayer is that as you walk through this experience together, you will grow in your heart for the Lord and for one another. Most importantly, you will discover your particular mission as a Christian. I hope that you delight to share your thoughts and needs with one another so that you will grow up into Christlikeness. Your safe little community becomes like fertile soil…a great place for your heart to develop like a well-watered plant!

This guide is written for use with the book, *Becoming a Healthy Disciple* (2013). It is best if every member of the small group read along in the chapters designated before each session. The material contained in the book will enhance your discussion and provide launching points into other areas of mutual concern and edification.

Be sure to come to each session fully prepared to enter into dialogue with your fellow pilgrims…the road ahead will be filled with both smooth travel conditions as well as some occasional potholes. Entering into the small group prayerfully and expectantly will aid in the quality and depth of your shared experiences each meeting.

The structure presented in the following pages is user-friendly and applicable to a wide variety of groups. Feel free to adapt to the particular needs of your participants and support your leader as s/he facilitates your gatherings for fellowship, prayer, worship and discussion. May God be pleased to smile down on your group with His empowering presence, His gentle leading, and His Fatherly blessing.

Your Brother in Christ,

President, Leadership Transformations, Inc.
Author, *Becoming a Healthy Disciple*
www.leadershiptransformations.org

Introduction

The *Becoming a Healthy Disciple Small Group Study and Worship Guide* has been written for intentional, thoughtful, purposeful believers in Jesus Christ who desire to live as a beloved disciple. This guide is designed for use with a small group and follows a suggested outline based on a 90-minute session:

Gathering   10 minutes
> ...time to get acquainted and comfortable with one another.

Worship   20 minutes
> ...time to pray, sing and reflect around the biblical focus for the session.

Discussion   50 minutes
> ...time to discuss the chapter questions and field additional comments.

Prayer   10 minutes
> ...time to pray with and for one another in the application of the trait.

All sessions include information which complements the book, *Becoming a Healthy Disciple,* and provides for a complete discussion of each trait. Feel free to adapt along the way and become creative in the execution of all sessions. The goal is to discuss all ten traits of a vital Christian within the context of a safe and affirming environment, which is bathed in prayer, deepened in worship, and surrounded by the strength and quality of healthy Christian relationships.

Your mission...as a leader and/or participant...is to discover the traits that are your strengths (for which you give God the glory!) and to identify the traits that you need to focus on in the near and distant future. Since becoming a healthy disciple is at its core a matter of the heart, it is essential that you treat this experience as a spiritual exercise… one which will draw you closer to the heart of God in order to listen for His still, small voice which beckons you to a deeper walk of faith.

You will notice that selected hymns and readings are used in the prayer and worship sections of each session. I am indebted to the team who put together *The Celebration Hymnal,* from which the hymns have been taken, and to Bishop Rueben P. Job who authored all of the reflective readings (excerpts from his Upper Room publication, *Guide to Prayer for All Who Seek God)*. Both of these resources have been significantly used of the Lord in my own personal prayer journey and I offer them in hopes they will be an encouragement to you. Special thanks to many friends and colleagues who suggested that this small group guide be written, and to the team at Leadership Transformations for their prayerful support.

My Small Group

Name	Phone Number	E-mail address

1 _____

2 _____

3 _____

4 _____

5 _____

6 _____

7 _____

8 _____

9 _____

10 _____

11 _____

12 _____

"It is only because he became like us that we can become like him."

-- Dietrich Bonhoeffer

1 Experiencing God's Empowering Presence

Study Section

The healthy disciple understands the role of the Holy Spirit and lives daily with a fresh reality of his power and presence.

"But the Counselor, the Holy Spirit, whom the Father will send in my name, will teach you all things and will remind you of everything I have said to you." (John 14:26)

Christians have all sorts of excuses for not getting involved in ministry opportunities…

- I should have shared my faith with my co-worker, but I didn't want to offend her;
- I could have joined the short-term mission team, but I don't have the time;
- I would have helped out by teaching the Sunday school class, but I don't feel comfortable working with children.

The shoulda-coulda-woulda litany of excuses we espouse show us how little we depend upon the ministry of the Holy Spirit. Jesus promised to send the Holy Spirit to all believers of every generation. The best part of the promise is that He delivered on it!

So, take time today to invite the ministry of the Holy Spirit to reside within you and watch how His gifts unfold and His fruit emerges right before your very eyes. No more excuses…because with the Holy Spirit's empowerment you too can live more abundantly!

Guidelines for This Session

Gathering

Congratulations! This is your first session as a small group, gathered to discuss *Becoming a Healthy Disciple*. After a time of casual fellowship, be sure everyone has introduced themselves, with basic remarks about their family, vocation, why they joined the group, and what they hope to get out of this study. Use an opening question such as, "What are you looking forward to in our times together?" or "In one word or phrase, how would you describe your understanding of disciple or discipleship?"

Worship

A guide to "Prayer and Worship" is provided for you following the prayer section below. Invite your group to participate in this theme-based small group worship experience. Your time in the Word, in song, in prayer, and in listening to reflective readings, will prepare you for your time of small group discussion. As you worship together, anticipate the fresh empowerment of God's Spirit and delight in His presence!

Discussion

In order to begin discussing trait one, "Experiences God's Empowering Presence," take a few minutes to review the contents of the chapter. Encourage group members to share what they consider to be the strong points of the chapter. Ask them to share how God used this material to affirm or challenge them in their personal spiritual life this past week. Include in your overview the biblical reflections from the Gospel of John and the five major sub-topics contained in the chapter...

1.1 – Exemplify His Fruit
1.1 – Embody His Thumbprint
1.1 – Express His Gifts
1.1 – Envision His Call
1.1 – Experience His Presence

Use the following questions for additional group reflection and renewal…

1. Which aspect of the ministry of the Holy Spirit needs further clarification for you today? Which aspect was most striking to you in this chapter and why?

    _____

    _____

    _____

    _____

2. How will you focus your heart and mind on the fruit of the Spirit in the coming week? Memorize the nine lovely fruit of the Spirit and place them in written form prominently before you in one or more creative locations in your home or office.

    _____

    _____

    _____

    _____

3. What gifts of the Spirit are you most thankful for today, and how will you hone your gift(s) in the days ahead? What gifts can you affirm in others?

    _____

    _____

    _____

    _____

4. Write out a prayer that speaks to how the Spirit is nudging you today to practice living your life in his empowering presence.

    _____

    _____

    _____

5. Share one or more highlights of this chapter with someone you trust, and commit to praying for one another for the faithful embodiment of this trait of discipleship health.

    _____

    _____

    _____

Prayer

Since this is your first session in this material, you may want to invite everyone to read together the Disciple's Prayer found on page 41 of *Becoming a Healthy Disciple*. Or, ask for volunteers to close your session with prayers for one another that focus on your discussion or specific requests presented by group members.

Encourage one another to read the following chapter in *Becoming a Healthy Disciple* in anticipation of the next study and worship session. Before dismissal, be sure to confirm the date and time of your next gathering!

1 Experiencing God's Empowering Presence

Prayer and Worship Section

Opening Prayer

Worship Song – *"Great Is Thy Faithfulness"* (The Celebration Hymnal, 139)

> Great is Thy faithfulness, O God, my Father,
> There is no shadow of turning with Thee.
> Thou changest not; Thy compassions, they fail not.
> As Thou hast been Thou forever wilt be.
>
> Great is Thy faithfulness! Great is Thy faithfulness!
> Morning by morning new mercies I see;
> All I have needed Thy hand hath provided.
> Great is Thy faithfulness, Lord, unto me!
>
> Summer and winter, and springtime and harvest,
> Sun, moon and stars in their courses above,
> Join with all nature in manifold witness
> To Thy great faithfulness, mercy and love.
>
> Pardon for sin and a peace that endureth,
> Thy own dear presence to cheer and to guide.
> Strength for today, and bright hope for tomorrow,
> Blessings all mine with ten thousand beside!

Scripture – John 14:16-21, 23-24

"I will ask the Father, and He will give you another Counselor to be with you forever – the Spirit of truth. The world cannot accept Him, because it neither sees Him nor knows Him. But you know Him, for He lives with you and will be in you. I will not leave you as orphans; I will come to you. Before long, the world will not see Me anymore, but you will see Me. Because I live, you also will live. On that day you will realize that I am in My Father, and you are in Me, and I am in you. Whoever has My commands and obeys them, he is the one who loves Me. He who loves Me will be loved by My Father, and I too will love him and show Myself to him.

If anyone loves Me, he will obey My teaching. My Father will love him, and We will come to him and make Our home with him. He who does not love Me will not obey My teaching. These words you hear are not My own; they belong to the Father who sent Me. The Counselor, the Holy Spirit, will teach you all things."

Reflection

"Most of us have lived long enough to have thought or said, 'I could never do that!' It is a common response of ordinary people like us to a task that seems to demand extraordinary wisdom, strength, or faith. However, the Bible is filled with stories of those who told God they could not lead, witness, or perform the task they were asked to do. Of course they were right! They could not do the difficult – or even the simple and easy – on their own. The biblical stories from Abraham to the first-century Christians point out that only with power from beyond themselves could the faithful fulfill their calling.

What are you planning to do that you cannot possibly achieve without help from beyond yourself? What do you feel God is calling you to be and do that is impossible without God's intervention in your life? These questions move us quickly to the realization that we often live our lives on the easy path of the least faith and effort. To observe the church is to see that we are not alone in choosing the easy path. Yet we know there is a better way and a higher calling for us as individuals, as congregations, and as denominations.

The early disciples were told to wait upon God until the power came. They waited and the power did come. The book of Acts is a brief record of how the early church carried on its life and ministry with power from beyond itself. The record of individuals and Christian movements that have transformed the world within and around them is testimony to their capacity to receive power from beyond themselves to fulfill their calling. This power was given to ordinary people who were called to live in an extraordinary way. Could that be your calling today?"

Rueben P. Job
Guide to Prayer for all who Seek God (219, 220)

Prayers for one another

Worship Song – *"Breathe on Me, Breath of God"* (The Celebration Hymnal, 393)

Breathe on me, Breath of God, fill me with life anew,
That I may love what Thou dost love, and do what Thou wouldst do.

Breathe on me, Breath of God, until my heart is pure,
Until with Thee I will one will, to do and to endure.

Breathe on me, Breath of God, till I am wholly Thine,
Until this earthly part of me Glows with Thy fire divine.

Breathe on me, Breath of God, so shall I never die,
But live with Thee the perfect life of Thine eternity.

Closing Prayer

2 Engaging in God-Exalting Worship

Study Section

The healthy disciple engages wholeheartedly in meaningful, God-focused worship experiences on a weekly basis with the family of God.

"The true worshipers will worship the Father in spirit and truth, for they are the kind of worshipers the Father seeks." (John 4:23)

"I didn't get anything out of that service" mumbled Wally the worshiper as he and his wife, Wanda, drove away from church.

Sound a tad familiar? Then you too might be entering worship with the wrong motivation. If Wally and Wanda were true worshipers, they would understand that worship is about giving, not getting.

The amazing reality, however, is that in giving we receive. Funny how that happens, isn't it? As we give ourselves back to God, he fills us with his joy. As we offer our lives as a living sacrifice, God blesses us for our obedience to his call. As we sing and pray and listen and serve, the bounty of his eternal rewards are overwhelming.

Next Sunday, enter the sanctuary with a heart's desire to do nothing but give. You will undoubtedly be amazed by how the Father's heart will sing over you with joy. In the meantime, pray that your daily time of worship will prepare you for weekly worship with the family of God!

Guidelines for This Session

Gathering

In this session, we pick up where we left off with our discussion of the ministry of the Holy Spirit and move into the subject of worship. After a casual time of getting reacquainted, invite the group to gather in a circle to commence the study. In this session, you may wish to talk about one of your most meaningful worship experiences – either at church, or on retreat, camping, or at a conference. As each person describes this event, focus on why the worship was so significant.

Worship

A guide to "Prayer and Worship" is provided for you following the prayer section below. Invite your group to participate in this theme-based small group worship experience. Your time in the Word, in song, in prayer, and listening to reflective readings, will prepare you for your time of small group discussion. As you worship together, anticipate the fresh empowerment of God's Spirit and delight in His presence! God desires to bless your shared experience as you talk about this important trait of healthy discipleship.

Discussion

In order to begin discussing trait two, "Engages in God Exalting Worship," take a few minutes to review the contents of the chapter. Encourage group members to share what they consider to be the strong points of the chapter. Ask them to share how God used this material to affirm or challenge them in their personal spiritual life this past week. Include in your overview the biblical reflections from the Gospel of John and the five major sub-topics contained in the chapter…

  2.1 – Preparation Begins on Monday
  2.2 – Participation Begets Fulfillment
  2.3 – Proclamation Styles Reflect Diversity
  2.4 – Protection from Distraction
  2.5 – Prescription for Enhancement

Use the following questions for additional group reflection and renewal...

1. What is the 'beautiful gift' you can give to God in worship this next week? How will your approach to congregational worship be different than it has been before?

    _____

    _____

    _____

    _____

2. In what ways can you encourage full engagement in God exalting worship among the members of your congregation in the days ahead?

    _____

    _____

    _____

    _____

3. What is your potential for distraction in worship and what choices can you make to radically alter the manner in which you approach worship fully focused on God rather than the needs and opportunities all around you?

    _____

    _____

    _____

    _____

4. Are there one or two things you can do this coming week that will encourage a deeper level of commitment among members of your local church?

    _____

    _____

    _____

    _____

5. With which of the five worship praxis principles do you resonate the most and why?

    _____

    _____

_____

_____

6. How can you reclaim the priority of Sabbath for yourself and your family? What will this mean regarding the activities which tend to engulf and consume any sense of consistent, weekly Sabbath rest?

_____

_____

_____

_____

Prayer

The Disciple's Prayer on page 59 of *Becoming a Healthy Disciple* can serve as your closing prayer if read together in unison. Otherwise, if group members wish to pray together in a more spontaneous fashion, that should be encouraged. Be sure to close your session in prayer regardless of the style of prayer chosen.

Encourage one another to read the following chapter in *Becoming a Healthy Disciple* in anticipation of the next study and worship session. Before dismissal, be sure to confirm the date and time of your next gathering!

2   Engaging in God-Exalting Worship

Prayer and Worship Section

Opening Prayer

Worship Song – *"Holy, Holy, Holy"* (The Celebration Hymnal, 3)

Holy, holy, holy! Lord God Almighty
Early in the morning our song shall rise to Thee.
Holy, holy, holy! Merciful and mighty!
God in three Persons, blessed Trinity!

Holy, holy, holy! All the saints adore Thee,
Casting down their golden crowns around the glassy sea.
Cherubim and seraphim falling down before Thee,
Which wert, and art, and evermore shalt be.

Holy, holy, holy! Though the darkness hide Thee,
Though the eye of sinful man Thy glory may not see.
Only Thou art holy – there is none beside Thee,
Perfect in power, in love, in purity.

Holy, holy, holy! Lord God Almighty!
All Thy works shall praise Thy name in earth, and sky, and sea.
Holy, holy, holy! Merciful and mighty!
God in three Persons, blessed Trinity!

Scripture – Calls to Worship (The Celebration Hymnal, 238) Read responsively

Come, let us sing for joy to the Lord; let us shout aloud to the Rock of our salvation. Let us come before Him with thanksgiving and extol Him with music and song. (Psalm 95: 1-2)

> *Come, let us bow down in worship, let us kneel before the Lord our Maker; for He is our God and we are the people of His pasture, the flock under His care. (Psalm 95: 6-7)*

Shout for joy to the Lord, all the earth. Worship the Lord with gladness; come before Him with joyful songs. Know that the Lord is God. It is He who made us, and we are His; we are His people, the sheep of His pasture. (Psalm 100 :1-3)

> *Enter His gates with thanksgiving and His courts with praise; give thanks to Him and praise His name. For the Lord is good and His love endures forever; His faithfulness continues through all generations. (Psalm 100: 4-5)*

Be still and know that I am God. I will be exalted among the nations;
I will be exalted in the earth. (Psalm 46:10)

> ***A time is coming and has now come when the true worshipers will worship the Father in spirit and truth, for they are the kind of worshipers the Father seeks. God is spirit, and His worshipers must worship in spirit and truth. (John 4: 23-24)***

Reflection

"What has your attention at this very moment? This reading? Perhaps, but we all know that we can give modest attention to several things at once. We eat, read, and listen for the phone all at the same time. When our search for something consumes all our energy and all our faculties, everything else fades away and disappears. Even a ringing phone goes unanswered when we are seeking to give answer to another call deep within. What are you searching for that consumes all your energy and attention? The quest for God is a search worthy of such all-consuming passion and energy. The biblical record indicates that such a search is always generously rewarded.

Jesus asked two of John's disciples (John 1:38) what they were looking for and invited them to come and see where and how he lived. The desire to know and be near to God has been placed within as an invitation to a lifelong quest for companionship with the divine. And yet, from personal experience we know that sometimes we look in all the wrong places. These disciples of Jesus were invited to continue their search where Jesus was and not where he was not. Our directions are certainly as plain as theirs are.

What are you looking for today and where will your search be successful? The quest for God is always successful when carried out where God is to be found. Where shall we begin the search? The deep inner rooms of our own soul, sacred scriptures, the book of history, current events, the lives of the saints, the poor and oppressed seeking our compassion, and the creation itself offer places where God has been most readily found in the past. Today pay attention to what has your undivided attention and follow the clues to a closer walk with God."

Rueben P. Job
A Guide to Prayer for all who Seek God (375,376)

Prayers for one another

Worship Song – "Be Thou My Vision" (The Celebration Hymnal, 562)

1. Be Thou my Vision, O Lord of my heart; Naught be all else to me, save that Thou art- Thou my best thought, by day or by night, Waking or sleeping, Thy presence my light.

2. Be Thou my Wisdom, and Thou my true Word; I ever with Thee and Thou with me, Lord; Thou my great Father, I Thy true son, Thou in me dwelling, and I with Thee one.

3. Riches I heed not, nor man's empty praise, Thou mine inheritance, now and always; Thou and Thou only, first in my heart, High King of heaven, my treasure Thou art.

4. High King of heaven, my victory won, May I reach heaven's joys, bright heaven's Sun! Heart of my own heart, what ever be-fall, Still be my Vision, O Ruler of all.

Closing Prayer

3 Practicing the Spiritual Disciplines

Study Section

The healthy disciple pursues the daily disciplines of prayer, Bible study, and reflection in the quietness of one's personal prayer closet.

"Remain in me, and I will remain in you." (John 13:4)

Lesser priorities tugging for our affection (and time) often usurp intimacy with Christ. Those alternative intimacies include climbing the corporate ladder; seeking self-fulfillment through money, sex, or influence over others; and a host of other ambitions and desires. All of them keep us from pursuing the heart of God.

When's the last time you sat quietly and reflectively in the presence of God? How long did you linger in his presence? For most Christians, practicing the spiritual disciplines feels like more work, another item to check off the daily to-do list. Don't let that happen to you.

God isn't any different from human parents. What he most longs for is an intimate relationship with all his children. The spiritual disciplines of prayer, Scripture study and reflection lead us into a deeper love of our Father. Make that your number one priority each new day and everything else will fall into place.

Today as you pray, sit a few minutes longer than usual and in the silence of the moment ask Jesus to help you keep intimacy with him your central mission in life. That's how your heart will become Christ's home today.

Guidelines for This Session

Gathering

This third session will focus on the subject of intimacy with Christ. After the group has gathered for some informal fellowship, invite them to sit in a circle for the entire session. An introductory question for this session should focus on the disciplines of prayer, Bible study and reflection. Ask participants to share answers to the question, "Why is cultivating a center of quiet so challenging for you today?" This will foster honest reflection throughout this important lesson.

Worship

A guide to "Prayer and Worship" is provided for you following the prayer section below. Invite your group to participate in this theme-based small group worship experience. Your time in the Word, in song, in prayer, and in listening to reflective readings, will prepare you for our time of small group discussion. As you worship together, anticipate the fresh empowerment of God's Spirit and delight in His presence!

Discussion

In order to begin discussing trait three, "Practices the Spiritual Disciplines," take a few minutes to review the contents of the chapter. Encourage group members to share what they consider to be the strong points of the chapter. Ask them to share how God used this material to affirm or challenge them in their personal spiritual life this past week. Include in your overview the biblical reflections from the Gospel of John and the five major sub-topics contained in the chapter...

    3.1 – Prayer: ACTS and Relate
    3.2 – Scripture: Read and Discover
    3.3 – Reflection: Review and Preview
    3.4 – Proactivity: Rhythm and Rhyme
    3.5 – Accountability: Family and Friends

Use the following questions for additional group reflection and renewal…

1. In the Gospel of John there are several places where Jesus demonstrates his priorities for his disciples through his life and his teachings. Note the following references in John 14-17 which highlight his role as spiritual mentor to his disciples. As you prayerfully read through each passage, begin to identify ways in which his priorities as noted are applicable to the life of a healthy disciple today.
    -   In John 14: 1-10 Jesus guides his disciples to the Father.
    -   In John 14: 15-17 Jesus points them to the Holy Spirit.
    -   In John 14: 1-3 and 14:27 Jesus encourages them with hope for tomorrow.
    -   In John 15: 18 and 16: 1-4, 32-33 Jesus speaks honestly of the messiness of the real world.
    -   In John 16:8 Jesus tells the truth about the human heart.
    -   In John 16:5 Jesus creates readiness for the already present activity of the Holy Spirit.
    -   In John 17:1-26 Jesus practices the ministry of prayer for his followers. His attention to their spiritual growth does not end when their time together is over but continues onward through prayer.

    _____
    _____
    _____
    _____

2. What spiritual disciplines are you in need of reprioritizing in your life, and how will you accomplish the goal of maintaining these disciplines in your daily walk with Christ?

    _____
    _____
    _____
    _____

3. Who do you need to invite into your life as a spiritual friend to hold you accountable for the practicing of your daily disciplines? Who around you needs this same kind of loving attention, and how will you prayerfully offer yourself for this purpose in his or her life?

_____

_____

_____

_____

Prayer

The Disciple's Prayer on page 83 of *Becoming a Healthy Disciple* can serve as your closing prayer if read together in unison. Otherwise, if group members wish to pray together in a more spontaneous fashion using the ACTS prayer method, that should be encouraged. Be sure to close your session in prayer regardless of the style of prayer chosen.

Encourage one another to read the following chapter in *Becoming a Healthy Disciple* in anticipation of the next study and worship session. Before dismissal, be sure to confirm the date and time of your next gathering!

3 Practicing the Spiritual Disciplines

Prayer and Worship Section

Opening Prayer

Worship Song – *"How Great Thou Art"* (The Celebration Hymnal, 147)

O Lord, my God, when I in awesome wonder
Consider all the wo rlds Thy hands have made,
I see the stars, I hear the rolling thunder,
Thy power throughout the universe displayed.

Then sings my soul, my Savior God to Thee;
How great Thou art! How great Thou Art! (repeat)

When through the woods and forest glades I wander
And hear the birds sing sweetly in the trees,
When I look down from lofty mountain grandeur,
And hear the brook and feel the gentle breeze.

And when I think that God, His Son not sparing,
Sent Him to die, I scarce can take it in;
That on the cross, my burden gladly bearing,
He bled and died to take away my sin.

When Christ shall come with shouts of acclamation
And take me home, what joy shall fill my heart!

Then I shall bow in humble adoration
And there proclaim: my God, how great Thou art!

Scripture – John 15: 1-17 (invite one person to read from their Bible)

- Remain in me, and I will remain in you..
- Love each other as I have loved you…
- You did not choose me, but I chose you to go and bear fruit – fruit that will last!

Reflection

"There was a light drizzle in the air as I walked along a darkening road, hands in my pockets, head down, thinking of a task I was to do and quite oblivious to the world around me. Suddenly a voice called my name. My head came up, I looked around, and there spotted a friend who was driving by and had stopped his car to greet me. We were several thousand miles from my home and a hundred miles from his. I suspect much of my life has been like that, preoccupied with personal issues and oblivious to the voice of God calling to me every day and in every circumstance.

The Bible and saints who have gone before us give ample evidence of God's consistent call to each of us. The Bible and the saints who have traveled this road before us also make clear the universal nature of God's call to all humankind. No one is left out, exempted, or overlooked. All are of equal worth and all are called. While we may think of certain vocations as callings, God appears to consider all of life as our calling, and that includes every honorable vocation.

Regularly practicing disciplines of the holy life puts us in position to hear God's call clearly. Those disciplines include prayer, fasting, community and personal worship, acts of mercy and compassion, and faithful living.

Hearing is an important step in saying yes to God's call. But once we hear, we must still decide whether we will go where invited or sent. In other words, hearing may be the easy part of saying yes to God's call. Once we have heard and counted the cost the most difficult task remains. However, with deep faith in the living God who calls us, the only reasonable response is to say yes. For in our best moments, we know God will ask us, only us, to say yes to an invitation that is right and good for us. Listen closely, think deeply, pray fervently, and you will be lead to the right answer to God's invitational call. In my experience the right answer is always yes. The good news is that even when I was unable to give the right answer, God was patient and gave me opportunity to grow in faith until I was able to say yes and to claim another part of my inheritance as a child of God."

Rueben P. Job
A Guide to Prayer for All Who Seek God (81, 82)

Prayers for one another

Worship Song – "*It Is Well With My Soul*" (The Celebration Hymnal, 705)

When peace like a river attendeth my way, When sorrows like sea billows roll; Whatever my lot, Thou hast taught me to say, "It is well, it is well with my soul."

It is well (it is well), with my soul (with my soul), It is well, it is well with my soul.

Though Satan should buffet, though trials should come, let this blessed assurance control, That Christ hath regarded my helpless estate, and hath shed His own blood for my soul.

My sin-O, the bliss of this glorious thought, My sin not in part, but the whole, Is nailed to the cross, and I bear it no more,

Praise the Lord, praise the Lord, O my soul.

And, Lord, haste the day when the faith shall be sight,
The clouds be rolled back as a scroll,
The trump shall resound and the Lord shall descend,
"Even so" it is well with my soul.

Closing Prayer

4 Learning and Growing in Community

Study Section

The healthy disciple is involved in spiritual and relational growth in the context of a safe and affirming group of like-minded believers.

"When they did (obey Jesus), they were unable to haul the net because of the large number of fish." (John 21:6)

Did you ever wonder why God placed so many "one anothers" in the Bible? The New Testament exhorts us to love one another, confess our sins and pray for one another, care for and greet and encourage and bear with and serve one another (just to name a few). Could it be quite possibly that God actually intended for faith communities to learn to live out the "one anothers" today? Absolutely!

When disciples obey Jesus together, "hauling the net" is nothing short of pure joy. When the church learns how to fulfill all the "one anothers" in the context of healthy environments for spiritual growth, then the world will come to know the Savior for real.

Commit today to improving the health of your spiritual life by growing up into Christlikeness in unity with your brothers and sisters in the faith. Ask God to lead you into an affirming group of believers who will hold you accountable for obedience to Christ. Mutual accountability—remember the "one anothers"—is the key to discovering the joy of journeying in community.

Guidelines for This Session

Gathering

This session will focus on the fourth trait of a healthy disciple, learning and growing in community. After a time of casual fellowship, invite the group to gather again in a circle for this session of worship and study. An opening question to consider would be, "In your experience as a believer, how have you most recently experienced authentic community?" It would also be helpful if your group talked about defining Christian community and their expectations for living out the one another's in the context of a safe environment.

Worship

A guide to "Prayer and Worship" is provided for you following the prayer section below. Invite your group to participate in this theme-based small group worship experience. Your time in the Word, in song, in prayer, and listening to reflective readings, will prepare you for your time of small group discussion. As you worship together, anticipate the fresh empowerment of God's Spirit and delight in His presence! God desires to bless your shared experience as you talk about this important trait of healthy discipleship.

Discussion

In order to begin discussing trait four, "Learns and Grows in Community," take a few minutes to review the contents of the chapter. Encourage group members to share what they consider to be the strong points of the chapter. Ask them to share how God used this material to affirm or challenge them in their personal spiritual life this past week. Include in your overview the biblical reflections from the Gospel of John and the five major sub-topics contained in the chapter...

   4.1 – Safe Place to Share
   4.2 – Safe Place to Pray
   4.3 – Safe Place to Process
   4.4 – Safe Place to Care
   4.5 – Safe Place to Grow

Use the following questions for additional group reflection and renewal…

1. Read through John 20 and 21. Note all the ways that Jesus appeared after his resurrection. What were some of the themes of these encounters with the risen Christ and how did his followers learn and grow in community as a result? Spend some time in these chapters, reflecting prayerfully on the life-changing impact that occurred as a result of faith communities coming into direct contact with Christ. How should these experiences impact your own community in the days ahead?

    _____

    _____

    _____

    _____

2. Are the small groups within your local church healthy? If not, how can you encourage health in these contexts of learning and growth?

    _____

    _____

    _____

    _____

3. How do you define the word *safe* in relation to small community groups? Do you concur with the five principles above and would you add any additional principles to the list? If there are groups within your fellowship that are no longer safe, what can you do to help bring health and vitality back into those groups?

    _____

    _____

    _____

    _____

Prayer

The Disciple's Prayer on page 103 of *Becoming a Healthy Disciple* can serve as your closing prayer if read together in unison. Otherwise, if group members wish to pray together in a more spontaneous fashion, that should be encouraged. Be sure to close your session in prayer regardless of the style of prayer chosen.

Encourage one another to read the following chapter in *Becoming a Healthy Disciple* in anticipation of the next study and worship session. Before dismissal, be sure to confirm the date and time of your next gathering!

4 Learning and Growing in Community

Prayer and Worship Section

Opening Prayer

Worship Song – *"We Are God's People"* (The Celebration Hymnal, 399)

We are God's people, the chosen of the Lord,
Born of His Spirit, established by His Word.
Our cornerstone is Christ alone, and strong in Him we stand;
O let us live transparently and walk heart to heart and hand in hand.

We are God's loved ones, the Bride of Christ, our Lord,
For we have known it, the love of God outpoured.
Now let us learn how to return the gift of love once given;
O let us share each joy and care and live with a zeal that pleases Heav'n.

We are the Body of which the Lord is Head,
Called to obey Him, now risen from the dead.
He wills us to be a family diverse, yet truly one;
O let us give our gifs to God and so shall His work on earth be done.

We are a Temple, the Spirit's dwelling place,
Formed in great weakness, a cup to hold God's grace.
We die alone, for on its own each ember loses fire;
Yet joined in one the flame burns on to give warmth and light and to inspire.

Scripture – John 21:1-14

Afterward Jesus appeared again to his disciples, by the Sea of Tiberias. It happened this way: Simon Peter, Thomas (called Didymus), Nathanael from Cana in Galilee, the sons of Zebedee, and two other disciples were together. "I'm going out to fish," Simon Peter told them, and they said, "We'll go with you." So they went out and got into the boat, but that night they caught nothing Early in the morning, Jesus stood on the shore, but the disciples did not realize that it was Jesus. He called out to them, "Friends, haven't you any fish?"

"No," they answered. He said, "Throw your net on the right side of the boat and you will find some." When they did, they were unable to haul the net in because of the large number of fish.

Then the disciple whom Jesus loved said to Peter, "It is the Lord!" As soon as Simon Peter heard him say, "It is the Lord," he wrapped his outer garment around him (for he had taken it off) and jumped into the water. The other disciples followed in the boat, towing the net full of fish, for they were not far from shore, about a hundred yards. When they landed, they saw a fire of burning coals there with fish on it, and some bread. Jesus said to them, "Bring some of the fish you have just caught."

Simon Peter climbed aboard and dragged the net ashore. It was full of large fish, 153, but even with so many the net was not torn. Jesus said to them, "Come and have breakfast." None of the disciples dared ask him, "Who are you?" They knew it was the Lord. Jesus came, took the bread and gave it to them, and did the same with the fish. This was now the third time Jesus appeared to his disciples after he was raised from the dead.

Reflection

"Jesus lived his life in community. From his childhood with Mary and Joseph to his calling and traveling with the disciples to his declaration that he and the Father were one, Jesus lived in community. A community of faith nurtured him, supported him, and informed him ("Who do the crowds say that I am?" [Luke 9:18]). It is unthinkable that we would try to live a faithful life without the gifts offered in a faithful community of Jesus. Jesus was known for valuing solitude since he retired to rest and pray, but living in community also marked his life.

Jesus makes a dramatic and revolutionary promise when he says, "Where two or three gather in my name, I am there among them" (Matt. 18:20). This is a welcome promise to those who may wonder if God is present in their lives or their affairs. This is a hopeful promise for those who sometimes feel alone and forsaken. This is an enormous assurance for those who face the unknown and need companionship and community.

We can be sure that Jesus keeps his promise and that when we gather in his name, he will be with us. We are often blessed by being in community. We receive encouragement, guidance, comfort, and hope by participating in a community. We often find our faith strengthened in community. These gifts of community are available to us all, and we receive them more readily when we remember that Jesus meets us there."

Rueben P. Job
A Guide to Prayer for All Who Seek God (227,228)

Prayers for one another

Worship Song–"*The Church's One Foundation*"(The Celebration Hymnal, 401)

The Church's one foundation is Jesus Christ, her Lord;
She is His new creation by water and the Word:
From heav'n He came and sought her to be His holy bride;
With his own blood He bought her, and for her life He died.

Elect from every nation, yet one o'er all the earth,
Her charter of salvation: One Lord, one faith, one birth;
One holy name she blesses, partakes one holy food;
And to one hope she presses, with every grace endued.

'Mid toil and tribulation and tumult of her war,
She waits the consummation of peace forevermore;
Till with the vision glorious her longing eyes are blest,
And the great Church victorious shall be the Church at rest.

Yet she on earth hath union with God, the Three in One,
And mystic, sweet communion with those whose rest is won:
O happy ones and holy! Lord, give us grace that we
Like them, the meek and lowly, on high may dwell with Thee.

Closing Prayer

5 Committing to Loving and Caring Relationships

Study Section

The healthy disciple prioritizes the qualities of relational vitality that lead to genuine love for one another in the home, workplace, church, and community.

"This is my commandment, that you love one another as I have loved you. No one has greater love than this, to lay down one's life for one's friends." (John 15:12-13)

Genuinely loving relationships cannot exist unless people can resolve conflicts. How do you deal with conflict? For many, the response of choice is to "sweep it under the carpet" and pretend it never occurred. But that only creates a bumpy carpet in the body of Christ—not safe for the Christian walk.

Far too many relationships are filled with painful, unresolved conflicts. Forgiveness is a topic of understanding but little application. However, the only way to begin sweeping out the bumps from under the carpet is to confess our sin and seek the forgiveness of others.

If you desire to embody the abundant life of Jesus Christ, then your relationships with others need to be genuinely loving and life-giving. Hard hearts that are unwilling to seek and offer forgiveness will not receive God's mercy and forgiveness. Ask God to lead you to those you have hurt—or who have hurt you—and begin the process of reconciliation today. Do this and your walk through life will be smoother—guaranteed.

Guidelines for This Session

Gathering

This session will deal with our commitment to loving and caring relationships. Often the barrier to healthy relationships is when we allow conflict to go unresolved. As the group gathers for the session, invite members to share with one another how their family of origin dealt with conflict. For some, there will be healthy examples to share, while the majority will discover that conflict was difficult to handle. Since this is the fifth session in this series, it will be important to remain sensitive to each other as the sharing continues.

Worship

A guide to "Prayer and Worship" is provided for you following the prayer section below. Invite your group to participate in this theme-based small group worship experience. Your time in the Word, in song, in prayer, and listening to reflective readings, will prepare you for your time of small group discussion. As you worship together, anticipate the fresh empowerment of God's Spirit and delight in His presence! God desires to bless your shared experience as you talk about this important trait of healthy discipleship.

Discussion

In order to begin discussing trait five, "Commits to Loving and Caring Relationships," take a few minutes to review the contents of the chapter. Encourage group members to share what they consider to be the strong points of the chapter. Ask them to share how God used this material to affirm or challenge them in their personal spiritual life this past week. Include in your overview the biblical reflections from the Gospel of John and the five major sub-topics contained in the chapter...

5.1 – Agape Love
5.2 – Absolute Joy

5.3 – Affirming Communication
5.4 – Resolving Conflict
5.5 – Additional Time
Use the following questions for additional group reflection and renewal…

An anonymous email arrived via cyberspace that caught my attention. It's included here as an appropriate reflection exercise for contemplating the roots and models of our healthiest relationships:

"Can you name the five wealthiest people in the world? The last five Heisman trophy winners? The last five winners of the Miss America contest? Five people who have won the Nobel or Pulitzer Prize? Five Academy Award winners for best actor or actress? The last decade's worth of World Series winners?

Very few of us remember the headlines of yesterday. These are no second-rate achievers. They're the best in their fields. But the applause dies. Awards tarnish. Achievements are forgotten. Accolades and certificates are buried with their owners.

Consider another quiz. You are guaranteed to do better on this one!

1. List a few teachers who aided your journey through school.

_____

_____

_____

_____

2. Name three friends who have helped you through a difficult time.

_____

_____

_____

_____

3. Name five people who have taught you something worthwhile.

    _____

    _____

    _____

    _____

4. Think of a few people who have made you feel appreciated and special.

    _____

    _____

    _____

    _____

5. List five people you enjoy spending time with.

    _____

    _____

    _____

    _____

6. Name a half dozen heroes whose stories have inspired you.

    _____

    _____

    _____

    _____

A little easier than the first set of questions? The lesson here is that the people who make a difference in your life aren't the ones with the most credentials, the most money, or the most awards. They're the ones who care and love and pour courage into your heart."

Commit to becoming that kind of person *today*. Don't forget to complete the quiz above! In fact, you may want to add this list of key people in your life to your prayer journal. And, by all means, be sure to write a note of thanks to as many of them as possible so that they hear how they brought a commitment to loving and caring relationships to life for you!

Repentance exercise. With whom do you need to resolve a long-standing or short-term conflict? Pause and pray and ask God to direct you to specific ways you can approach this person with a genuine apology, seek their forgiveness, and restore the relationship with love and caring. Don't allow the Judas-in-you to cloud what God would desire most—Jesus-in-you!

Prayer

The Disciple's Prayer on page 124 of *Becoming a Healthy Disciple* can serve as your closing prayer if read together in unison. Otherwise, if group members wish to pray together in a more spontaneous fashion, that should be encouraged. Be sure to close your session in prayer regardless of the style of prayer chosen.

Encourage one another to read the following chapter in *Becoming a Healthy Disciple* in anticipation of the next study and worship session. Before dismissal, be sure to confirm the date and time of your next gathering!

5 Committing to Loving and Caring Relationships

Prayer and Worship Section

Opening Prayer

Worship Song – *"Fairest Lord Jesus"* (The Celebration Hymnal, 87)

Fairest Lord Jesus; Ruler of all nature,
O Thou of God and man the Son.
Thee will I cherish; Thee will I honor,
Thou my soul's glory, joy, and crown.

Fair are the meadows; Fairer still the woodlands,
Robed in the blooming garb of spring.
Jesus is fairer; Jesus is purer,
Who makes the woeful heart to sing.

Fair is the sunshine; Fairer still the moonlight
And all the twinkling starry host.
Jesus shines brighter; Jesus shines purer
Than all the angels heav'n can boast.

Beautiful Savior! Lord of the nations!
Son of God and son of man!
Glory and honor, praise, adoration,
Now and forevermore be Thine!

Scripture – John 15:9-17 (invite one person to read from their Bible)

Reflection

"As I drove up the driveway, our children raced out the front door and met me at the car. Before I could get my suitcase out of the car, they were telling me about Puddles, the dog that had followed them home from the little store a few blocks away. We had talked nearly every day about the dog we were going to get when we were able to move into the country. Everyone wanted a big dog like a Dalmatian or a black Labrador. But as I got out of the car I noticed a dog that was small and scraggly, of mixed origin, very soon to be a mother, and yet very personable. The chorus of affirmation for the dog from our children was compelling. But I gave no clear answer to their question, "Can we keep Puddles?" I did not want to adopt a dog like this, and I knew I had to move quickly to make sure we did not have a dog and a litter of puppies on our hands.

I suggested that after our evening meal and our chores were completed we would talk about what to do with the dog. Later, when we were all settled in the family room, and with the dog in the garage, I asked each of the children to tell me why he or she thought we should keep Puddles when we could get a beautiful and large dog. Each of them had a good reason. She needed a home. We would enjoy the puppies. She would be a watchdog. Last I turned to our eight-year-old son and asked him what we should do with the dog and why. His eyes filled with tears and he said, "We should keep her." I asked him for his reason why we should keep this scraggly dog. He responded through his tears, "Because she loves me." We kept Puddles. She was with us while our children grew up and when they called home from college and career, their first question was always, "How is Puddles?" She lived with us seventeen years because one little boy loved her enough to save her.

Jesus knew that only love was strong enough to keep the disciples faithful in the days ahead. His repeated questions to Peter were meant to clarify for Peter what the real love of his life was. Only love is strong enough to keep us faithful, and the question to us from the One who loves us without condition or qualification is first of all about our love. For God knows what we know: Only love is strong enough to keep us faithful…and joyful. May our love for God continue to grow in the presence of God's love for us."

Rueben P. Job
A Guide to Prayer for All Who Seek God (191,192)

Prayers for one another

Worship Song – "*My Jesus I love Thee*" (The Celebration Hymnal, 79)

My Jesus, I love Thee; I know Thou art mine.
For Thee all the follies of sin I resign.
My gracious Redeemer, my Savior art Thou:
If ever I loved Thee, my Jesus, 'tis now.

I love Thee because Thou hast first loved me
And purchased my pardon on Calvary's tree.
I love Thee for wearing the thorns on Thy brow.
If ever I loved Thee, my Jesus, 'tis now.

I'll love Thee in life; I will love Thee in death
And praise Thee as long as Thou lendest me breath.
And say when the death dew lies cold on my brow,
"If ever I loved Thee, my Jesus, 'tis now."

In mansions of glory and endless delight,
I'll ever adore Thee in heaven so bright.
I'll sing with the glittering crown on my brow,
"If ever I loved Thee, my Jesus, 'tis now."

Closing Prayer

6 Exhibiting Christlike Servanthood

Study Section

The healthy disciple practices God-honoring servanthood in every relationship context of life and ministry.

"I have set you an example that you should do as I have done for you." (John 13:15)

Many Christians today serve others in order to be seen and acknowledged. Are you looking for some well-deserved applause for your most recent act of kindness? Think you should have received a thank-you note for visiting that shut-in? Waiting to hear your name from the pulpit as the key individual who made your church ministry a reality?

Guess what? Give it up! It's best if you wait no longer. If your motivation for serving others is to be recognized for your generosity, then any ounce of sacrifice related to your service is gone.

When Jesus embodied the "full extent of his love" for his disciples, it was behind closed doors where no one else could see. And his act of kindness was demonstrated in the holding and washing of his disciples' feet, the lowliest of servant-worthy jobs.

Serving like Jesus means that we are willing to help others for their sake, and not our own. His example is not glamorous, but gracious and generous and godly. In your prayers today, invite Jesus to give you a loving heart to serve others in a hidden, anonymous, and sacrificial way.

Guidelines for This Session

Gathering

Exhibiting Christlike servanthood is the topical focus of this session. After a time of informal conversation, invite the group to gather for study and worship. A suggested introductory question for consideration is, "In what practical ways have you been served by another in this past week? What did it feel like to be on the receiving end of service?" Serving others pleases the Lord and the act of service toward another is the way in which we extend the love of Christ. As a small group, the goal during this session is to encourage one another in our acts of service.

Worship

A guide to "Prayer and Worship" is provided for you following the prayer section below. Invite your group to participate in this theme-based small group worship experience. Your time in the Word, in song, in prayer, and listening to reflective readings, will prepare you for your time of small group discussion. As you worship together, anticipate the fresh empowerment of God's Spirit and delight in His presence! God desires to bless your shared experience as you talk about this important trait of healthy discipleship.

Discussion

In order to begin discussing trait six, "Exhibits Christlike Servanthood," take a few minutes to review the contents of the chapter. Encourage group members to share what they consider to be the strong points of the chapter. Ask them to share how God used this material to affirm or challenge them in their personal spiritual life this past week. Include in your overview the biblical reflections from the Gospel of John and the five major sub-topics contained in the chapter...

    6.1 – A Towel and Basin
    6.2 – A Servant's Heart

6.3 – A Willingness to Give and Receive
6.4 – A Listening Ear
6.5 – A Life Well Lived

Use the following questions for additional group reflection and renewal…

1. In this past week, how have others blessed you in their service in your behalf? List the many ways you've been served, and note especially the names of the individuals who gave of themselves for you. What can you do in this coming week to express your gratitude for their service?

_____

_____

_____

_____

2. As you read through the anonymous poem "Dying to Self," what images came to mind that reflect an embodiment of these principles within you and others in the Christian community? How are these examples of servanthood "God sightings" in your midst?

_____

_____

_____

_____

3. Read Romans 12:9-13. How does this paragraph reflect the servanthood principle of being "givers more than takers?"

_____

_____

_____

_____

4. Read Romans 12:14-16. How do these verses reflect the servanthood principle of being "listeners more than talkers?"

_____

_____

_____

_____

5. Read Romans 12:17-18. How do these verses reflect the servanthood principle of being "peace-makers more than trouble makers?"

_____

_____

_____

_____

6. How would you assess the status of your servant heart today? What cleansing and restorative work needs to be done within you in order for you to become a healthier servant of Christ, exhibiting his heart, attitude and behavior in the coming week/month/year?

_____

_____

_____

_____

7. Write out a prayer to the Lord focusing on your thoughts from the above questions and reflections.

_____

_____

_____

_____

Prayer

The Disciple's Prayer on page 144 of *Becoming a Healthy Disciple* can serve as your closing prayer if read together in unison. Otherwise, if group members wish to pray together in a more spontaneous fashion, that should be encouraged. Be sure to close your session in prayer regardless of the style of prayer chosen.

Encourage one another to read the following chapter in *Becoming a Healthy Disciple* in anticipation of the next study and worship session. Before dismissal, be sure to confirm the date and time of your next gathering!

6 Exhibiting Christlike Servanthood

Prayer and Worship Section

Opening Prayer

Worship Song – "*I Surrender All*" (The Celebration Hymnal, 596)

All to Jesus I surrender, all to Him I freely give;
I will ever love and trust Him, in His presence daily live.

I surrender all, I surrender all.
All to Thee, my blessed Savior, I surrender all.

All to Jesus I surrender, humbly at His feet I bow,
Worldly pleasures all forsaken, take me, Jesus, take me now.

All to Jesus I surrender, make me, Savior, wholly Thine;
May thy Holy Spirit fill me, may I know Thy power divine.

All to Jesus I surrender, Lord, I give myself to Thee;
Fill me with Thy love and power, let Thy blessing fall on me.

Scripture – John 13:1-17

It was just before the Passover Feast. Jesus knew that the time had come for him to leave this world and go to the Father. Having loved his own who were in the world, he now showed them the full extent of his love.

The evening meal was being served, and the devil had already prompted Judas Iscariot, son of Simon, to betray Jesus. Jesus knew that the Father had put all things under his power, and that he had come from God and was returning to God; so he got up from the meal, took off his outer clothing, and wrapped a towel around his waist. After that, he poured water into a basin and began to wash his disciples' feet, drying them with the towel that was wrapped around him.

He came to Simon Peter, who said to him, "Lord, are you going to wash my feet?" Jesus replied, "You do not realize now what I am doing, but later you will understand." "No," said Peter, "you shall never wash my feet." Jesus answered, "Unless I wash you, you have no part with me." "Then, Lord," Simon Peter replied, "not just my feet but my hands and my head as well!"

Jesus answered, "A person who has had a bath needs only to wash his feet; his whole body is clean. And you are clean, though not every one of you." For he knew who was going to betray him, and that was why he said not every one was clean.

When he had finished washing their feet, he put on his clothes and returned to his place. "Do you understand what I have done for you?" He asked them. "You call me Teacher and Lord, and rightly so, for that is what I am. Now that I, your Lord and Teacher, have washed your feet, you also should wash one another's feet. I have set you an example that you should do as I have done for you. I tell you the truth, no servant is greater than his master, nor is a messenger greater than the one who sent him. Now that you know these things, you will be blessed if you do them."

Reflection

"Being a disciple was becoming stressful. The pace clearly had quickened during this three-year course in discipleship. The crowds had grown larger and demanded more. The lessons to be learned often seemed over the heads of the disciples. Jesus talked more and more about his own death and what was to follow. Frankly the disciples did not understand it, and the more confused they became, the more frustrated they became. We can appreciate that phenomenon. It happens to us. When we are under a heavy load for a long period of time, we often become frustrated, impatient, and sometimes not very nice to be around. We even begin to compare ourselves to others and begin to think that we deserve a little bigger slice of the reward pie than even our closest friend.

That kind of reaction to stress may explain why the disciples began arguing about who was to be regarded as the greatest among those who followed Jesus. Jesus shattered their hopes of achieving special status or special reward (Luke 22:26).

The world's system of reward has nothing to do with the disciple's system of reward. A disciple of Jesus Christ is called first to be servant of all, and the leader is to take the lowliest position of service. This system turns the world's concept of leadership upside down. The first disciples found it hard to understand and even more difficult to live by such a value system. But Jesus seems to say there is no other way. Disciples serve."

Rueben P. Job
A Guide to Prayer for All Who Seek God (129, 130)

Prayers for one another

Worship Song – *"Take My Life and Let It Be Consecrated"* (The Celebration Hymnal, 597)

Take my life and let it be – consecrated, Lord, to Thee;
Take my moments and my days – let them flow in ceaseless praise, let them flow in ceaseless praise.

Take my hands and let them move – at the impulse of Thy love;
Take my feet and let them be, swift and beautiful for Thee, swift and beautiful for Thee.
Take my voice and let me sing – always, only, for my King;
Take my lips and let them be filled with messages from Thee, filled with messages from Thee.

Take my silver and my gold – not a mite would I withhold;
Take my intellect and use every power as Thou shalt choose, every power as
Thou shalt choose.

Take my love, my Lord, I pour – at Thy feet its treasure store;
Take myself and I will be ever only, all for Thee, ever only all for Thee.

Take my will and make it Thine – it shall be no longer mine;
Take my heart it is Thine own, it shall be Thy royal throne, it shall be
Thy royal throne.

Closing Prayer

7 Sharing the Love of Christ Generously

Study Section

A healthy disciple maximizes every opportunity to share the love of Christ, in word and deed, with those outside the faith.

"For God so loved the world that he gave his one and only Son, that whoever believes in him shall not perish but have eternal life." (John 3:16)

What do you think makes Jesus smile? I believe it's when he sees his children loving God, loving neighbors as we love ourselves, and loving the world he gave his life to redeem—all through a love defined by our words and deeds.

The gospel of our Lord can be summarized in one word: Love. Not a syrupy kind of love that's short-lived, but an agape kind of love that's eternal. Sharing God's powerful, life-changing, no-matter-what kind of love is the mandate set before us.

Who in your world needs some serious loving today? It may be your spouse who misses your tenderness, or your child who longs for your attentiveness, or your friend who desires your closeness, or your neighbor who waits for your witness . . . or the lost, lonely, or least who are dying and in need of your faithfulness.

Your outward focus of love is a reflection of your inward journey of joy. Ask Jesus to remove barriers that would restrict you from loving today. This will certainly make him smile!

Guidelines for This Session

Gathering

The outward nature of the disciple...via evangelism, social concern, and international missions...is the focus of our session. After the group gathers for study and worship, ask members to share about a person they know who isn't walking with God today. It is with that person in mind that each participant is invited to share in this session. The kingdom of God is advanced as we partner with the Lord in generously loving others in the name of Jesus. Be sure to remind one another of the person they have named and by the end of the session identify ways to begin to prayerfully reach out to them.

Worship

A guide to "Prayer and Worship" is provided for you following the prayer section below. Invite your group to participate in this theme-based small group worship experience. Your time in the Word, in song, in prayer, and listening to reflective readings, will prepare you for your time of small group discussion. As you worship together, anticipate the fresh empowerment of God's Spirit and delight in His presence! God desires to bless your shared experience as you talk about this important trait of healthy discipleship.

Discussion

In order to begin discussing trait seven, "Shares the Love of Christ Generously," take a few minutes to review the contents of the chapter. Encourage group members to share what they consider to be the strong points of the chapter. Ask them to share how God used this material to affirm or challenge them in their personal spiritual life this past week. Include in your overview the biblical reflections from the Gospel of John and the five major sub-topics contained in the chapter...

7.1 – Evangelism
7.2 – Social Concern
7.3 – International Missions
7.4 – Diversity of Friendships
7.5 – Dispenser of Grace

Use the following questions for additional group reflection and renewal...

1. In what ways do you resonate with Nicodemus as a seeker, a law-focused inquirer, who was sensitized to the work of Jesus and was even tenderly and compassionately moved by the death of Jesus but had a hard time fully believing in him and accepting his love and leadership over his life?

   _____

   _____

   _____

   _____

2. Which of the three main areas of outreach (evangelism, social action, and international missions/relief and development) are your strongest? Which area needs some work and what can you do about making alterations in your lifestyle to accommodate the necessary changes?

   _____

   _____

   _____

   _____

3. How would you describe your circle of friendships today? With whom are you spending time that is stretching you to think about life and service to others in new and different ways? Are there people within your reach who are of different color, ethnicity, ability, or socioeconomic background with whom you can begin to spend time with in order to broaden your perspectives on the issues and needs of our world today? Who are they and how can you serve them?

   _____

   _____

   _____

   _____

4. In what practical ways can you be a dispenser of God's grace toward a family member, work associate, neighbor, or friend in this coming week without needing to receive anything in return? Try it and see how it changes your heart toward that person!

_____

_____

_____

_____

5. Can you articulate the essence of the gospel to a seeker? Are you able to succinctly share the main points of your personal testimony in two or three minutes? If not, please be sure to work on these and add them to your arsenal of tools that are ready for use at a moment's notice. You too are a part of the word-of-mouth revolution!

_____

_____

_____

_____

Prayer

The Disciple's Prayer on page 169 of *Becoming a Healthy Disciple* can serve as your closing prayer if read together in unison. Otherwise, if group members wish to pray together in a more spontaneous fashion, that should be encouraged. By now you have gotten to know one another more intimately and may wish to pray together in triads or pairs. Be sure to close your session in prayer regardless of the style of prayer chosen.

Encourage one another to read the following chapter in *Becoming a Healthy Disciple* in anticipation of the next study and worship session. Before dismissal, be sure to confirm the date and time of your next gathering!

7 Sharing the Love of Christ Generously

Prayer and Worship Section

Opening Prayer

Worship Song – *"All Hail the Power of Jesus' Name"* (The Celebration Hymnal, 43)

All hail the power of Jesus' name! Let angels prostrate fall;
Bring forth the royal diadem, and crown Him Lord of all (repeat).

Ye chosen seed of Israel's race, ye ransomed from the fall,
Hail Him who saves you by His grace, and crown Him Lord of all (repeat).

Let every kindred, every tribe on this terrestrial ball,
To Him all majesty ascribe, and crown Him Lord of all (repeat).

O that with yonder sacred throng we at His feet may fall!
We'll join the everlasting song, and crown Him Lord of all (repeat).

Scripture – John 3: 14-16, 36; 5:24; 10: 27-29; I John 5:11-13 (The Celebration Hymnal, 785)

"Life Everlasting"

And as Moses lifted up the serpent in the wilderness, even so must the Son of Man be lifted up, that whoever believes in Him should not perish but have eternal life.

For God so loved the world that He gave His only begotten Son, that whoever believes in Him should not perish but have everlasting life.

He who believes in the Son has everlasting life; and he who does not believe in the Son shall not see life, but the wrath of God abides on him.

Most assuredly, I say to you, he who hears My Word and believes in Him who sent Me has everlasting life, and shall not come into judgment, but has passed from death into life.

My sheep hear My voice, and I know them, and they follow Me. And I give them eternal life, and they shall never perish; neither shall anyone snatch them out of My hand.

My Father, who has given them to Me, is greater than all; and no one is able to snatch them out of My Father's hand.

And this is the testimony: that God has given us eternal life, and this life is in His Son.

He who has the Son has life; He who does not have the Son of God does not have life.

These things I have written to you who believe in the name of the Son of God, that you may know that you have eternal life, and that you may continue to believe in the name of the Son of God.

Reflection

"Jesus was often prompted by compassion to act on behalf of those who were suffering loss, disease, and hunger. It seems inevitable that those who follow Jesus must also show compassion in all of their decisions and actions. This is especially true of those who relate to people suffering hunger, disease, and death. The followers of Jesus cannot ignore the needy of the world, and neither can we look away from the needs of the world. If our lives are modeled after the one we claim to follow, we will, as Jesus did, look with compassion upon all who cross our paths. Looking with compassion requires the further step of seeking to alleviate the pain that prompted our compassion.

Colossians 3:12 has provided a source of guidance and strength for my life for many years. "As God's chosen ones, holy and beloved, clothe yourselves with compassion, kindness, humility, meekness, and patience." The author of Colossians calls the followers of Jesus to clothe themselves with these five incredible qualities, and the first of them is compassion. As chosen ones, it is the only option. To be chosen as God's beloved can only evoke gratitude and goodness. Therefore our response of compassion for the world is really a response to God's unqualified love for us. How could we respond in any other way?

Jesus saw a need, had compassion, then sought to remedy the need. As Christians we seek to model our lives after Jesus. The pain of the world draws forth our compassion and our effort to remedy the need. As God's beloved, pray this week for eyes to see the needs around you and for compassion that will prompt actions to meet those needs with loving remedy."

Rueben P. Job
A Guide to Prayer for All Who Seek God (349, 350)

Prayers for one another

Worship Song – "*Amazing Grace*" (The Celebration Hymnal, 343)

Amazing grace! How sweet the sound that saved a wretch like me!
I once was lost but now am found; was blind, but now I see.

'Twas grace that taught my heart to fear, and grace my fears relieved.
How precious did that grace appear the hour I first believed.

The Lord has promised good to me; His Word my hope secures.
He will my shield and portion be as long as life endures.

Thro' many dangers, toils, and snares I have already come.
'Tis grace hath brought me safe thus far, and grace will lead me home.

When we've been there ten thousand years, bright shining as the sun,
We've no less days to sing God's praise than when we'd first begun.

Closing Prayer

8 Managing Life Wisely and Accountably

Study Section

The healthy disciple develops personal life management skills and lives within a web of accountable relationships.

"As long as it is day, we must do the work of him who sent me." (John 9:4)

Stress is the word of our time. Everyone I know understands what the word means, because they embody the word in their lifestyle. Activities, responsibilities, relationships, to-do lists, and taking care of our "stuff" seem to preoccupy our every waking moment. Gone are the slow days of sauntering through life. Fast pace is here to stay.

Life management skills are needed now more than ever. They begin with knowing our personal mission and focus. They grow from there into defining our key relationships and specific responsibilities. They lead to a deep, internal understanding of what to say yes to and when to say no. All of this within a framework of accountable friendships, trusted confidantes who will help us maintain our God-defined priorities.

Tackling this trait of discipleship health is critical to our well-being. Otherwise, life will continue as a hectic treadmill, and we won't ever jump off to assess our direction. Pray today for a fresh vision for your overstressed life. Ask Jesus to help you embrace a life balanced in wisdom (intellectual), stature (physical), favor with God (spiritual) and favor with mankind (relational).

Guidelines for This Session

Gathering

This session will focus on how a disciple "manages life wisely and accountably" in the context of spiritual community. For the past seven sessions your group has been formed into a cohesive gathering of like-minded, like-hearted believers. After you enjoy some informal conversation and gather into a circle, consider asking one another, "What are the major stress points of your life today?" This will begin to identify the areas where God's transforming power can begin to work in each of your lives over the coming weeks and months. Practical, helpful ideas will be shared in this session.

Worship

A guide to "Prayer and Worship" is provided for you following the prayer section below. Invite your group to participate in this theme-based small group worship experience. Your time in the Word, in song, in prayer, and listening to reflective readings, will prepare you for your time of small group discussion. As you worship together, anticipate the fresh empowerment of God's Spirit and delight in His presence! God desires to bless your shared experience as you talk about this important trait of healthy discipleship.

Discussion

In order to begin discussing trait eight, "Manages Life Wisely and Accountably," take a few minutes to review the contents of the chapter. Encourage group members to share what they consider to be the strong points of the chapter. Ask them to share how God used this material to affirm or challenge them in their personal spiritual life this past week. Include in your overview the biblical reflections from the Gospel of John and the five major sub-topics contained in the chapter…

    8.1 – Mission, Roles, and Goals
    8.2 – Balanced Lifestyle

8.3 – Stress Reduction and Management
8.4 – Accountable Relationships
8.5 – Nine No's for Every One Yes

Use the following questions for additional group reflection and renewal…

1. This chapter included several exercises for your consideration. For example:
   a. Writing a mission statement (eight steps recommended in the text).
   b. Outline personal roles and goals.
   c. Identify areas of stress and ways to manage/eliminate stress—beginning today!

   Complete as many of these as possible, and share them with a friend or with members of your small group.

   _____

   _____

   _____

   _____

2. Read John 9. What is the gift that the blind man received from Jesus in verses 1-12? What is the reaction of the Pharisees in verses 13-34? What conclusions can you glean from the final paragraph in verses 35-41 about spiritual blindness and the need for God's gift of spiritual eyesight?

   _____

   _____

   _____

   _____

3. How can you help a fellow disciple in the pursuit of his or her personal mission as "a work of God on display" in the coming week?

   _____

   _____

   _____

   _____

4. Review the mission statements of Jesus (John 6:38; John 10:10; John 18:37; Mark 10:45; Luke 19:10). How do these statements inspire the management of your life with wisdom and accountability; and, how do they affect the development of your own mission statement?

_____

_____

_____

_____

5. Write out a prayer asking God to help you balance the multiple demands upon you during this season of life and service.

_____

_____

_____

_____

Prayer

The Disciple's Prayer on page 193 of *Becoming a Healthy Disciple* can serve as your closing prayer if read together in unison. Otherwise, if group members wish to pray together in a more spontaneous fashion, that should be encouraged. Be sure to close your session in prayer regardless of the style of prayer chosen.

Encourage one another to read the following chapter in *Becoming a Healthy Disciple* in anticipation of the next study and worship session. Before dismissal, be sure to confirm the date and time of your next gathering!

8 Managing Life Wisely and Accountably

Prayer and Worship Section

Opening Prayer

Worship Song – *"Have Thine Own Way, Lord"* (The Celebration Hymnal, 591)

> Have Thine own way, Lord! Have Thine own way!
> Thou art the Potter; I am the clay.
> Mold me and make me after Thy will,
> While I am waiting, yielding and still.

> Have Thine own way, Lord! Have Thine own way!
> Search me and try me, Master, today.
> Whiter than snow, Lord, wash me just now,
> As in Thy presence humbly I bow.

> Have Thine own way, Lord! Have Thine own way!
> Wounded and weary, help me, I pray.
> Power, all power surely is Thine!
> Touch me and heal me, Savior divine!

> Have Thine own way, Lord! Have Thine own way!
> Hold o'er my being absolute sway!
> Fill with Thy Spirit till all shall see
> Christ only, always living in me!

Scripture – John 9:1-5; 2:13-16 (invite one or two to read from their Bible)

Reflection

"So many of the entries in my journal end, "I am yours." It appears so often because that is the way I want to live my life every day. It is also there because I know how easily I am distracted to "belong" to something or someone else. I genuinely want to belong to God fully and without qualification. But living in our culture, we easily tend to brush aside that desire.

Mary made this incredible leap of faith and offered herself without qualification to God for whatever God chose to bring into her life. At the moment of this confession, recorded in Luke 1:38, she could not have known the magnitude of her decision. Yes, the angel messenger was clear in reporting God's desire for her, but it was still a huge step to say a willing and faithful yes to whatever God would choose. The risk to her reputation, the commitment of faith to an unknown path, the simple trust that God would provide today and tomorrow were not unlike the ingredients of our decision to offer ourselves to God without qualification.

In our better moments we know that it makes little difference what others may think of us. We know deep within our hearts that pleasing God is far more important than pleasing those around us. And yet risking our reputation for God is difficult for us. It is easy to remain silent and hidden when my colleagues make decisions based on the cultural norms rather than in the way of Christ. I don't like being called "too spiritual" or "unrealistic," and so I'm tempted to remain silent when I should speak a clear and simple word of faith. Yes, "I am yours." Help me to live that way.

We like to think we can know the future, and so we make plans, make investments, and seek to determine what the future will be. Planning, investing, and preparing are wonderful practices that we should incorporate in our lives. However, these practices should not dull our readiness to hear God's call to an unknown path and our readiness to say yes to that call. "I am yours." Lead me always in your path.

We know we are entirely dependent upon God, yet we forget and try to make our own provision for tomorrow or waste our energy in anxiety and fear that we will be forsaken when tomorrow comes. Mary was able to trust her life fully to the everlasting arms, sure that she would be upheld no matter what the future brought. "I am yours." Help me to remember you provided for me as a helpless baby; you provide for me now and will provide for me through eternal ages. Help me to live as one life totally given to you."

Rueben P. Job
A Guide to Prayer for All Who Seek God (41, 42)

Prayers for one another

Worship Song – *"May the Mind of Christ, My Savior"* (The Celebration Hymnal, 568)

> May the mind of Christ, my Savior, live in me from day to day,
> By His love and pow'r controlling all I do and say.
>
> May the Word of God dwell richly in my heart from hour to hour,
> So that all may see I triumph only thro' His pow'r.
>
> May the peace of God my Father rule my life in everything,
> That I may be calm to comfort sick and sorrowing.
>
> May the love of Jesus fill me as the waters fill the sea;
> Him exalting, self abasing—this is victory.
>
> May I run the race before me, strong and brave to face the foe,
> Looking only unto Jesus as I onward go.
>
> May His beauty rest upon me as I seek the lost to win;
> And may they forget the channel, seeing only Him.

Closing Prayer

9 Networking with the Body of Christ

Study Section

The healthy disciple actively reaches out to others within the Christian community for relationships, worship, prayer, fellowship, and ministry.

"May they be brought to complete unity to let the world know that you sent me and have loved them even as you have loved me." (John 17:23)

Unity. A small word with gigantic meaning. The implications of genuine spiritual unity are in direct proportion to the fulfillment of Jesus' prayer for building the kingdom of God. Jesus wants us to take part in building his kingdom. It will require that we participate prayerfully in uniting the people of God.

Unity. For Jesus' disciples, it was essential that they embrace one another's differences of background and vocation. Why would it be any different today? He's not asking us to water down the gospel in order to have feel-good connections with the diversity of all who claim to be Christians without solid biblical theology. He's inviting us to network with those who share our convictions and embody the Great Commission (Matt. 28:16-20).

Unity. If Jesus made it the focus of this chapter-long prayer (John 17), we should certainly make it a part of our prayer today. Ask God to give you a heart to discover the richness of the diversity of the body of Christ. This will lead us all into greater unity.

Guidelines for This Session

Gathering

Unity is a theme that is close to the heart of God and needs to be reflected in our walk with God – together. You've experienced significant unity in your small group experiences during this series of worship and discussions. After you gather in your circle, begin by thanking God for the spiritual unity provided by His Spirit. Ask each participant to share one way in which that unity has been demonstrated in the times you've shared as a group. This will provide an excellent segue into the following moments of prayer and worship.

Worship

A guide to "Prayer and Worship" is provided for you following the prayer section below. Invite your group to participate in this theme-based small group worship experience. Your time in the Word, in song, in prayer, and listening to reflective readings, will prepare you for your time of small group discussion. As you worship together, anticipate the fresh empowerment of God's Spirit and delight in His presence! God desires to bless your shared experience as you talk about this important trait of healthy discipleship.

Discussion

In order to begin discussing trait nine, "Networks with the Body of Christ," take a few minutes to review the contents of the chapter. Encourage group members to share what they consider to be the strong points of the chapter. Ask them to share how God used this material to affirm or challenge them in their personal spiritual life this past week. Include in your overview the biblical reflections from the Gospel of John and the five major sub-topics contained in the chapter...

  9.1 – Diversity of Connection
  9.2 – Holy Dissatisfaction
  9.3 – Cross-Cultural Pollination

9.4 – Multidenominational Investigation
9.5 – Prayerful Participation

Use the following questions for additional group reflection and renewal…

1. List here the diversity of your existing relationships. Start with those
   you know in a general sense; and then write down those who you know
   who are within the family of God. How can you foster new relationships
   with others in the Christian community who are more diverse and can
   enhance your understanding of the unity of the body of Christ?

   _____

   _____

   _____

   _____

2. When is the last time you participated in a worship service that was
   different from your norm? Jot down observations about the unique
   elements of that worship service. In what ways did the diversity of the
   body of Christ express itself in that worship service? Describe how that
   service helped you engage at a deeper level with true, God-exalting
   worship?

   _____

   _____

   _____

   _____

3. As you review your personal prayer journal, how much diversity is
   expressed on the pages before you? In what ways can you expand the
   direction of your prayers on behalf of the larger body of Christ?

   _____

   _____

   _____

   _____

4. In the coming year, where can you go within the body of Christ to grow
   your connections with other ethnic communities or your experiences
   of multi-denominational relationships? Who within your existing

fellowship or small group can travel this new relationship journey with you and hold you accountable to taking this step forward?

_____

_____

_____

_____

5. What ministry opportunities can you take advantage of in the coming year that will take you into new arenas of service for the sake of sharing the gospel and expanding the kingdom of God? Explore and select one or more, and watch how God expands your horizons for service within the body of Christ!

_____

_____

_____

_____

Prayer

The Disciple's Prayer on page 217 of *Becoming a Healthy Disciple* can serve as your closing prayer if read together in unison. Otherwise, if group members wish to pray together in a more spontaneous fashion, that should be encouraged. Be sure to close your session in prayer regardless of the style of prayer chosen.

Encourage one another to read the following chapter in *Becoming a Healthy Disciple* in anticipation of the next study and worship session. Before dismissal, be sure to confirm the date and time of your next gathering!

9 Networking with the Body of Christ

Prayer and Worship Section

Opening Prayer

Worship Song – *"O For A Thousand Tongues"* (The Celebration Hymnal, 21)

O for a thousand tongues to sing my great Redeemer's praise,
The glories of my God and King, the triumphs of His grace.

Jesus! The name that charms our fears, that bids our sorrows cease,
'Tis music in the sinner's ears, 'tis life and health and peace.

He breaks the pow'r of cancelled sin, He sets the prisoner free;
His blood can make the foulest clean, His blood availed for me.

Hear Him, ye deaf; His praise, ye dumb, your loosened tongues employ;
Ye blind, behold your Savior come; and leap, ye lame, for joy.

My gracious Master and my God, assist me to proclaim,
To spread thro' all the earth abroad, the honors of Thy name.

Scripture – John 17: 20-26

"My prayer is not for them alone. I pray also for those who will believe in me through their message, that all of them may be one, Father, just as you are in me and I am in you. May they also be in us so that the world may believe that you have sent me. I have given them the glory that you gave me, that they may be one as we are one: I in them and you in me. May they be brought to complete unity to let the world know that you sent me and have loved them even as you have loved me. "Father, I want those you have given me to be with me where I am, and to see my glory, the glory you have given me because you loved me before the creation of the world. "Righteous Father, though the world does not know you, I know you, and they know that you have sent me. I have made you known to them, and will continue to make you known in order that the love you have for me may be in them and that I myself may be in them."

Reflection

"Salvation is free, but the cost of discipleship is enormous. I try to hide from the truth, but when I read the Gospels and seek to live in communion with God, I discover both parts of the statement are dead-center truth. I can do nothing to earn my salvation. My redemption is a pure gift of grace, a gift offered to me without qualification or reservation. I am God's child and no one or no thing can change that fact. Jesus Christ lived, died, and lives again to bring this gift of salvation to me in all of its fullness. My faith can appropriate this gift, but even my greatest doubt cannot change its reality. I am God's beloved, embraced in God's love for now and eternity. All words are inadequate to describe the extravagance and grandeur of the gift of salvation. Our hymns of praise and gratitude fall lifeless before the immensity of his gift. We simply and humbly offer all that we are to the One who offers us the option of becoming more than we are.

In offering ourselves as fully as we can, we discover the cost of discipleship. For to bind our lives to Jesus Christ requires that we try to walk with him into the sorrows and suffering of the world. Being bound to Jesus Christ, we see barriers broken down and we are led to places we have never been before and to carry loads we have never even seen before. Having offered ourselves to Jesus Christ, we may expect to become the eyes, ears, voice, and hands of Jesus Christ in the world and in the church. The cost of salvation? It is completely free and without cost. The cost of discipleship? Only our lives—nothing more and nothing less."

Rueben P. Job
A Guide to Prayer for All Who Seek God (135, 136)

Prayers for one another

Worship Song – *"They'll Know We are Christians"* (The Celebration Hymnal, 429)

We are one in the Spirit; we are one in the Lord.
We are one in the Spirit; we are one in the Lord.
And we pray that all unity may one day be restored.

And they'll know we are Christians by our love, by our love.
Yes, they'll know we are Christians by our love.

We will walk with each other; we will walk hand in hand.
We will walk with each other; we will walk hand in hand.
And together we'll spread the news that God is in our land.

We will work with each other; we will work side by side.
We will work with each other; we will work side by side.
And we'll guard each one's dignity and save each one's pride.

All praise to the Father, from whom all things come.
And all praise to Christ Jesus, His only Son.
And all praise to the Spirit, who makes us one.

Closing Prayer

10 Stewarding a Life of Abundance

Study Section

The healthy disciple recognizes that every resource comes from the hand of God and is to be used generously for kingdom priorities and purposes.

"Unless a kernel of wheat falls to the ground and dies, it remains only a single seed. But if it dies, it produces many seeds." (John 12:24)

In this passage Jesus is reminding his hearers that for life to emerge in them, he himself first must be willing to die. Here's how to apply this truth: For the abundant life of Christ to be lived out in us, *we* must consistently die to ourselves. Dying to ourselves means that we freely release everything we have been given so others may discover life for themselves.

Are you willing to die to yourself? This is the road to eternal life, the avenue called "discipleship." Healthy disciples invite the life-transforming Christ to permeate every decision they make. When we invite Christ to live through us, we open-handedly steward or manage carefully every kernel of life entrusted to our care—not for our own sake, but for God's redemptive work to be accomplished in the hearts of others.

Seeding our daily life lovingly and generously with all the resources we have will lead to the abundant life of discipleship Jesus calls us to receive.

Guidelines for This Session

Gathering

Congratulations! You've made it to the tenth trait of a healthy disciple, "stewarding a life of abundance!" This session will wrap up the series and draw to conclusion what it means to become a spiritually healthy disciple of Jesus Christ. Be sure to celebrate what God has done in your midst throughout these ten gatherings. Discuss ways in which your group can continue to meet in the future. As an opening question to answer together, you may want to ask, "How has this series helped you define a life of discipleship and in what ways can we continue to encourage one another in our respective faith journeys?"

Worship

A guide to "Prayer and Worship" is provided for you following the prayer section below. Invite your group to participate in this theme-based small group worship experience. Your time in the Word, in song, in prayer, and listening to reflective readings, will prepare you for your time of small group discussion. As you worship together, anticipate the fresh empowerment of God's Spirit and delight in His presence! God desires to bless your shared experience as you talk about this important trait of healthy discipleship.

Discussion

In order to begin discussing trait ten, "Stewards a Life of Abundance," take a few minutes to review the contents of the chapter. Encourage group members to share what they consider to be the strong points of the chapter. Ask them to share how God used this material to affirm or challenge them in their personal spiritual life this past week. Include in your overview the biblical reflections from the Gospel of John and the five major sub-topics contained in the chapter...

10.1 – Serve Openhandedly
10.2 – Steward Prayerfully
10.3 – Sacrifice Financially
10.4 – Seed Generously
10.5 – Smile Abundantly

Use the following exercise for additional group reflection and renewal…

Stewarding a life of abundance means that we are willing to assess the true condition of our personal life stewardship in light of God's abundant gifts. For this final trait, the challenge for the disciple in pursuit of health and vitality is to begin to look carefully at the various stewardship issues raised in this chapter and move ahead in addressing each issue individually.

The following chart is designed to help you start working on each of these issues. As you edit and revise each category, share with others the direction you sense the Lord leading you in your desire to steward generously your life of abundance.

Take the time *now* to begin renewing a life of abundant stewardship. You will be so glad that you did!

Stewarding A Life of Abundance
By God's grace and guidance…

God's Abundance	My Stewardship (when, where, how)
Personal life mission (WHY)	
Personal roles in life (WHO)	
Personal goals for life (WHAT)	
Priorities for my schedule (TIME)	
Proactive seeding, serving, sacrifice (TALENT)	
Physical body (TEMPLE)	
Phinances (Finances!) (TREASURE)	
Prayerful joy! (TRUE HEART)	

Prayer

The Disciple's Prayer on page 238 of *Becoming a Healthy Disciple* can serve as your closing prayer if read together in unison. Otherwise, if group members wish to pray together in a more spontaneous fashion, that should be encouraged. Be sure to close your session in prayer regardless of the style of prayer chosen, especially since this is your final session in this study.

10   Stewarding a Life of Abundance

Prayer and Worship Section

Opening Prayer

Worship Song – *"Praise to the Lord, the Almighty"* (The Celebration Hymnal, 210)

> Praise to the Lord, the Almighty, the King of creation!
> O my soul, praise Him, for He is thy health and salvation!
> All ye who hear, now to His temple draw near;
> Join me in glad adoration!
>
> Praise to the Lord, who o'er all things so wondrously reigneth,
> Shelters thee under His wings, yea, so gently sustaineth!
> Hast thou not seen how thy desires all have been
> Granted in what He ordaineth?
>
> Praise to the Lord, who doth prosper thy work and defend thee;
> Surely His goodness and mercy here daily attend thee.
> Ponder anew what the Almighty can do
> If with His love He befriend thee.
>
> Praise to the Lord! O let all that is in me adore Him!
> All that hath life and breath, come now with praises before Him!
> Let the "amen" sound from His people again;
> Gladly forever adore Him!

Scripture – John 12: 23-26, 44-46

Jesus replied, "The hour has come for the Son of Man to be glorified. I tell you the truth, unless a kernel of wheat falls to the ground and dies, it remains only a single seed. But if it dies, it produces many seeds. The man who loves his life will lose it, while the man who hates his life in this world will keep it for eternal life. Whoever serves me must follow me; and where I am, my servant also will be. My Father will honor the one who serves me.

Then Jesus cried out, "When a man believes in me, he does not believe in me only, but in the one who sent me. When he looks at me, he sees the one who sent me. I have come into the world as a light, so that no one who believes in me should stay in darkness."

Reflection

"We could be very upset with millionaires who lived in life-robbing poverty because of ignorance or personal choice. We would be very disappointed in someone who had enormous wealth but refused to spend any of it for even the simple resources to sustain life. Why then are we not outraged about Christians by the millions who live as though God were dead and God's grace were exhausted? Could it be because we live that way so often ourselves?

The good news we share with one another is the gospel's declaration that no matter where we are in life, we are the recipients of God's limitless grace. We can have peace, joy, assurance, comfort, hope, tranquility, confidence, and companionship with our Creator and beyond that, life eternal. With a life bank full of such gifts we are indeed rich. And yet, so often I permit myself to slip into poverty thinking and poverty living. I feel anxious, alone, fearful, faithless, without joy, and sometimes without hope. I feel this way because I have forgotten and lost grip on the inheritance that God gives me anew every morning.

Many of us live in spiritual poverty because we have forgotten who we are as God's children and who God is as our loving and almighty Creator. The fact that you are reading these words suggests that you are reaching out even now to claim your full inheritance as a child of God. May God grant grace and wisdom to do so more and more today and every day of your life. Claim your inheritance and live as God's beloved child today."

Rueben P. Job
A Guide to Prayer for All Who Seek God (395, 396)

Prayers for one another

Worship Song – "*As the Deer*" (The Celebration Hymnal, 548)

As the deer panteth for the water, so my soul longeth after Thee.
You alone are my heart's desire and I long to worship Thee.

You alone are my strength, my shield;
To You alone may my spirit yield.
You alone are my heart's desire,
And I long to worship Thee.

You're my friend and You are my brother, even though You are a King.
I love You more than any other, so much more than anything.

I want You more than gold or silver, only You can satisfy.
You alone are the real joy-giver, and the apple of my eye.

Closing Prayer

Spiritual Health Check-up:
The Ten Traits of a Healthy Disciple

Instructions: On a scale of 0-2 (0=not a part of my experience today; 1=slightly a part of my experience today; 2=very much a part of my experience today), rate each of the following sub-points per trait. Add up your total points per trait and your overall score. Total possible points equals 100.

The healthy disciple is prayerful in all of the following aspects of personal life and ministry, is reliant upon God's power and the authority of His Word, and...

1. Experiences God's Empowering Presence – the healthy disciple understands the role of the Holy Spirit and lives daily with a fresh reality of his power and presence (John 14:26, "The Counselor, the Holy Spirit, will teach you all things and will remind you of everything I have said to you).

1.1	– Exemplify his fruit	0	1	2
1.2	– Embody his thumbprint	0	1	2
1.3	– Express his gifts	0	1	2
1.4	– Envision his call	0	1	2
1.5	– Experience his presence	0	1	2

Total for Trait One = _____

2. Engages in God-Exalting Worship – the healthy disciple engages whole-heartedly in meaningful, God-focused worship experiences on a weekly basis with the family of God (John 4:23, "The true worshipers will worship the Father in spirit and truth, for they are the kind of worshipers the Father seeks").

2.1	– Preparation begins Monday	0	1	2
2.2	– Participation begets fulfillment	0	1	2
2.3	– Proclamation styles reflect diversity	0	1	2
2.4	– Protection from distraction	0	1	2
2.5	– Prescription for enhancement	0	1	2

Total for Trait Two= _____

3.   Practices the Spiritual Disciplines – the healthy disciple pursues the daily
        disciplines of prayer, Bible study and reflection in the quietness of one's
        personal prayer closet (John 15:4, "Remain in me, and I will remain in you").

3.1	– Prayer: ACTS and Relate	0	1	2
3.2	– Scripture: Read and Discover	0	1	2
3.3	– Reflection: Review and Preview	0	1	2
3.4	– Proactivity: Rhythm and Rhyme	0	1	2
3.5	– Accountability: Family and Friends	0	1	2

Total for Trait Three = _____

4.   Learns and Grows in Community – the healthy disciple is involved in
        spiritual and relational growth in the context of a safe and affirming group
        of like-minded believers (John 21: 6, "When they did (obey Jesus), they
        were unable to haul the net because of the large number of fish").

4.1	– Safe place to share	0	1	2
4.2	– Safe place to pray	0	1	2
4.3	– Safe place to process	0	1	2
4.4	– Safe place to care	0	1	2
4.5	– Safe place to grow	0	1	2

Total for Trait Four = _____

5.   Commits to Loving and Caring Relationships – the healthy disciple
        prioritizes the qualities of relational vitality that lead to genuine love for one
        another in the home, workplace, church and community (John 15: 12,13,
        "This is my commandment, that you love one another as I have loved you.
        No one has greater love than this, to lay down one's life for one's friends").

5.1	– Agape love	0	1	2
5.2	– Absolute joy	0	1	2
5.3	– Affirming communication	0	1	2
5.4	– Resolving conflict	0	1	2
5.5	– Additional time	0	1	2

Total for Trait Five = _____

6.   Exhibits Christ-like Servanthood – the healthy disciple practices God-honoring servanthood in every relational context of life and ministry (John 13: 15, "I have set you an example that you should do as I have done for you").

6.1 – A towel and basin	0	1	2
6.2 – A servant's heart	0	1	2
6.3 – A willingness to give and receive	0	1	2
6.4 – A listening ear	0	1	2
6.5 – A life well lived	0	1	2

Total for Trait Six = _____

7.   Shares the Love of Christ Generously – the healthy disciple maximizes every opportunity to share the love of Christ, in word and deed, with those outside the faith (John 3: 16, "For God so loved the world that he gave his one and only Son, that whoever believes in him shall not perish but have eternal life").

7.1 – Evangelism	0	1	2
7.2 – Social concern	0	1	2
7.3 – International missions	0	1	2
7.4 – Diversity of friendships	0	1	2
7.5 – Dispenser of grace	0	1	2

Total for Trait Seven = _____

8.   Manages Life Wisely and Accountably – the healthy disciple develops personal life management skills and lives within a web of accountable relationships (John 9:4, "As long as it is day, we must do the work of him who sent me").

8.1 – Mission, roles and goals	0	1	2
8.2 – Balanced lifestyle	0	1	2
8.3 – Stress reduction and management	0	1	2
8.4 – Accountable relationships	0	1	2
8.5 – Nine No's for every One Yes	0	1	2

Total for Trait Eight = _____

9.   Networks with the Body of Christ – the healthy disciple actively reaches out to others within the Christian community for relationships, worship, prayer, fellowship, and ministry (John 17:23, "May they be brought to complete unity to let the world know that you sent me and have loved them even as you have loved me").

9.1	– Diversity of connection	0	1	2
9.2	– Holy dissatisfaction	0	1	2
9.3	– Cross-cultural pollination	0	1	2
9.4	– Multi-denominational investigation	0	1	2
9.5	– Prayerful participation	0	1	2

Total for Trait Nine = _____

10.   Stewards a Life of Abundance – the healthy disciple recognizes that every resource comes from the hand of God and is to be used generously for kingdom priorities and purposes (John 12:24, "Unless a kernel of wheat falls to the ground and dies, it remains only a single seed. But if it dies, it produces many seeds").

10.1	– Serve openhandedly	0	1	2
10.2	– Steward prayerfully	0	1	2
10.3	– Sacrifice financially	0	1	2
10.4	– Seed generously	0	1	2
10.5	– Smile abundantly…make Jesus smile!	0	1	2

Total for Trait Ten = _____

Grand Total = _____

After completing the self-assessment, answer the following questions:

1. Which are my strongest traits as a disciple of Christ?

   _____

   _____

   _____

   _____

2. Which traits do I need to prayerfully consider for further development?

   _____

   _____

   _____

   _____

3. What action steps can I take to strengthen my strengths and equip my developing areas in the near future?

   _____

   _____

   _____

Your growth plan needs to be bathed in prayer and sprinkled with Christian grace given in the context of your small group!

About the Author

Stephen A. Macchia is the founding president of Leadership Transformations, Inc. (LTI), a ministry focusing on the spiritual formation needs of leaders and the spiritual discernment processes of leadership teams in local church and parachurch ministry settings. In conjunction with his leadership of LTI, he also serves as the director of the Pierce Center for Disciple-Building at Gordon-Conwell Theological Seminary. He is the author of several books, including *Becoming a Healthy Church, Becoming a Healthy Disciple, Becoming A Healthy Team,* and *Crafting A Rule of Life.* Stephen and his wife, Ruth, are the proud parents of Nathan and Rebekah and reside in Lexington, Massachusetts.

For more information about Stephen A. Macchia or Leadership Transformations, Inc., visit:
www.LeadershipTransformations.org
www.HealthyChurch.net
www.RuleOfLife.com

Other Titles by Stephen A. Macchia

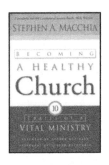

In **Becoming a Healthy Church**, Stephen A. Macchia illustrates how to move beyond church growth to church health. Healthy growth is a process that requires risk taking, lifestyle changes, and ongoing evaluation. This book is a practical, hands-on manual to launch you and your church into a process of positive change. Available in 3 Languages: English, Spanish, Korean.

Becoming a Healthy Disciple explores the ten traits of a healthy disciple, including a vital prayer life, evangelistic outreach, worship, servanthood, and stewardship. He applies to individual Christians the ten characteristics of a healthy church outlined in his previous book, Becoming a Healthy Church. Discipleship is a lifelong apprenticeship to Jesus Christ, the master teacher. Macchia looks to John the beloved disciple as an example of a life lived close to Christ.

Becoming a Healthy Disciple Small Group Study & Worship Guide is a companion to Steve Macchia's book, *Becoming a Healthy Disciple*. This small group guide provides discussion and worship outlines to enrich your study of the ten traits of a healthy disciple. This 12-week small group resource provides a Study, Worship, and Prayer guidelines for each session.

Becoming a Healthy Team is essential for building the kingdom. Stephen A. Macchia offers tried and tested principles and practices to help your leadership team do the same. He'll show you how to Trust, Empower, Assimilate, Manage, and Serve. That spells TEAMS and ultimately success. Filled with scriptural guideposts, Becoming a Healthy Team provides practical answers and pointed questions to keep your team on track and moving ahead.

In **Crafting a Rule of Life** Stephen A. Macchia looks to St. Benedict as a guide for discovering your own rule of life in community. It is a process that takes time and concerted effort; you must listen to God and discern what he wants you to be and do for his glory. But through the basic disciplines of Scripture, prayer and reflection in a small group context this practical workbook will lead you forward in a journey toward Christlikeness.

Additional Resouces @
SPIRITUALFORMATIONSTORE.COM

Guide to Prayer for All Who Walk With God

The latest from Rueben Job, A Guide to Prayer for All Who Walk With God offers a simple pattern of daily prayer built around weekly themes and organized by the Christian church year. Each week features readings for reflection from such well-known spiritual writers as Francis of Assisi, Teresa of Avila, Dietrich Bonhoeffer, Henri J. M. Nouwen, Sue Monk Kidd, Martin Luther, Julian of Norwich, M. Basil Pennington, Evelyn Underhill, Douglas Steere, and many others.

Guide to Prayer for All Who Seek God

For nearly 20 years, people have turned to the Guide to Prayer series for a daily rhythm of devotion and personal worship. Thousands of readers appreciate the series' simple structure of daily worship, rich spiritual writings, lectionary guidelines, and poignant prayers. Like its predecessors, A Guide to Prayer for All Who Seek God will become a treasured favorite for those hungering for God as the Christian year unfolds.

Guide to Prayer for Ministers and Other Servants

A best-seller for more than a decade! This classic devotional and prayer book includes thematically arranged material for each week of the year as well as themes and schedules for 12 personal retreats. The authors have adopted the following daily format for this prayer book: daily invocations, readings, scripture, reflection, prayers, weekly hymns, benedictions, and printed psalms.

Guide to Prayer for All God's People

A compilation of scripture, prayers and spiritual readings, this inexhaustible resource contains thematically arranged material for each week of the year and for monthly personal retreats. Its contents have made it a sought-after desk reference, a valuable library resource and a cherished companion.

LEADERSHIP
TRANSFORMATIONS INC.

FORMATION | DISCERNMENT | RENEWAL

- Soul Care Retreats and Soul Sabbaths
- Emmaus: Spiritual Leadership Communities
- Selah: Spiritual Direction Certificate Program
- Spiritual Formation Groups
- Spiritual Health Assessments
- Spiritual Discernment for Teams
- Sabbatical Planning
- Spiritual Formation Resources

Visit www.LeadershipTransformations.org
or call (877) TEAM LTI.

Made in the USA
Monee, IL
20 September 2022

14334930R00057